PARENThetically Speaking . . .

Kids can be too smart for their own good. You feed them, clothe them, teach them everything you know . . . and what happens? You wake up one morning and realize that what you have created is a miniature you. Good or bad—that's for you to decide.

Art Linkletter says that "kids say the darnest things." Larry Wilde proves that kids say the funniest things . . . and that parents are funny, too, and are really nothing but kids grown up.

After you read *your* side of the story turn this book over and hear what the kids have to say! Are they getting smarter? Or are you getting dumber? Or, are you (as usual) giving them the benefit of the doubt? After all, if they're so smart, maybe it's your fault!

THE OFFICIAL DUMB PARENTS JOKE BOOK

by Larry Wilde

PINNACLE BOOKS   LOS ANGELES

ABOUT THE AUTHOR

This eighth "Official" joke book represents a milestone in the unusually versatile career of Larry Wilde. With his book sales over 2,500,000, Wilde is now the architect of the largest selling humor series in the history of publishing.

Comedian Larry Wilde has entertained at America's leading hotels and nightclubs, while *actor* Larry Wilde is frequently seen on television commercials and on many of the situation comedy series (Mary Tyler Moore, Sanford and Son, and the like).

Born in Jersey City, New Jersey, Wilde served two years in the United States Marine Corps and has a bachelor's degree from the University of Miami, Florida.

Besides the Pinnacle joke book series, *author* Larry Wilde has penned articles for professional journals as well as *Gallery, Genesis, TV Guide, Penthouse, Coronet, Cosmo Forum,* and other popular magazines.

He is also the author of two serious works dealing with comedy technique: *The Great Comedians* (Citadel) and *How the Great Comedy Writers Create Laughter* (Nelson-Hall).

Larry is married to the former Maryruth Poulos and lives in Los Angeles where, between Las Vegas engagements and concert performances, as *lecturer* Larry Wilde, he delivers talks on humor. In addition, Wilde conducts a class in comedy at UCLA, where he is referred to on campus as *Professor* Larry Wilde.

CONTENTS

THE OFFICIAL
DUMB PARENTS
JOKE BOOK

GROWN-UP SIMPLETONS

Talbot and his son John were called to the teacher's office.

"Mr. Talbot," said the schoolmarm, "I asked John 'Who shot Abraham Lincoln?' and he said he didn't do it!"

"Well, teacher," said Talbot, "if my kid said he didn't do it—he didn't do it!"

They left the school and on their way home, Talbot turned to his boy and asked, "Tell me, son, did you do it?"

Son: Where are the Himalayas?

Pop: If you'd put things away, you'd know where to find them.

* * *

Junior was being chided for his low grades. Little Robert, who lived next door, was held up as an example. "Robert doesn't get C's and D's, does he?" asked his father.

"No, but he's different," Junior said. "He has smart parents!"

* * *

Ritter was seated in a cafeteria when a woman and two children sat down at his table and began to eat. Suddenly Ritter burped.

"Sir," said the woman haughtily, "are you in the habit of doing that before your children?"

"Dere are no rules in my house," replied Ritter. "Sometimes I go first, sometimes dey go first."

* * *

Teacher: Say, who did your homework?

Colin: My father.

Teacher: All alone?

Colin: No, I helped him with it!

2

"Honey," said Mrs. Stuart to her husband, "John's teacher says he ought to have an encyclopedia."

"Encyclopedia, my eye," exclaimed Mr. Stuart. "Let him walk to school like I did."

* * *

Aboard a coast-bound plane that made several intermediate stops, little Alice asked her mother, "What was the name of the city before last that we landed in?"

The mother, engrossed in a paperback, grumbled, "How do I know? And why do you suddenly want to know, anyhow?"

"Well, for one thing," observed Alice, "Papa got off there."

* * *

Grandma: How did Julian do on his history exam?
Mother: Oh, not at all well. But it wasn't his fault. Why, they asked him about things that happened before he was born!

* * *

Did you hear about the dumb father who got up and struck a match to see if he had blown out the candle?

Wife:	I had to marry you to find out how stupid you are.
Husband:	You should have known that the minute I asked you.

* * *

Old-fashioned Emmett approached Sandra's father, intent upon asking him for her hand in marriage.

"Sir," he blurted out, "I have an attachment for your daughter, and . . ."

"See here, young man," interrupted the parent, "when my daughter needs accessories, I'll buy them myself."

* * *

"Dad, why do you write so slow?" asked Dennis.

"I have to," replied his father. "I'm a slow reader."

* * *

Dean:	I hate to tell you this, Mr. Jones, but you son is a moron!
Jones:	What! Where is that young good-for-nothing? I'll teach him to join a fraternity without consulting me!

Did you hear about the minister who decided to brighten up Sunday school activities and give them more appeal for modern youth?

He installed a juke-box, a coffee-bar, and a discothèque, booked pop groups, let the boys and girls mix freely together, allowed them to smoke, and encouraged them to talk freely about their problems. Attendance dropped to nil.

Parents claimed that Sunday school was no fit place to send their children.

*　　*　　*

Son: What is an autobiography?
Father: Er, the story of an automobile.

*　　*　　*

"I gotta 'A' in spelling," Tony told his mother.

"You dope!" she replied. "There isn't any 'A' in spelling."

*　　*　　*

Did you hear about the dumb father who returned from lunch and saw a sign on his door, "Back in 30 minutes," so he sat down to wait for himself?

Talented TV comedy scribe Bill Dana contributed this titanic touch of tomfoolery:

Hugh and his parents were drinking at the bar in a train station when they heard a whistle. The three of them rushed out of the bar onto the platform only to discover that they'd missed the train.

"The next train is in one hour," said the stationmaster.

The three went back into the bar. The parents had another drink, Hugh had a Coke.

Again they heard a whistle, rushed out and discovered the train pulling away.

"Next one is sixty minutes from now!" said the stationmaster.

An hour later, Hugh, with mom and dad, raced out onto the platform, and his parents leaped onto the train as it pulled away. The boy was left standing on the platform and began to laugh uproariously.

"Your parents just left you," said the stationmaster. "Why are you laughing?"

"They came down to see me off!"

Little Boy: (calling father at office) : Hello, who is this?

Father: (recognizing son's voice) : The smartest man in the world.

Little Boy: Pardon me. I got the wrong number.

* * *

Harris took his son to see a show which featured fifty of the most daringly undressed girls in the country. "Phooey, phooey, phooey," Harris kept muttering.

"Whatsa matter, Pop? Don't you like the show?"

"Sure I do," he replied. "I was just thinking of your mother."

* * *

"Aren't you afraid the hot climate in India might disagree with your wife?"

"It wouldn't dare."

* * *

Mother: Were you the one who saved my little boy from drowning?

Lifeguard: Yes.

Mother: (angrily) : Well, where's his cap?

Marshall turned to his wife, who was sitting next to him, and said, "This train will soon go under a river."

She looked startled, then said, "Well, for goodness sake, don't just sit there—close the window."

* * *

"Been riding backwards for ten hours," Metcalf explained to his wife after he got off the train. "I never could stand that."

"Why," said his spouse, "didn't you ask the person sitting opposite to change seats with you?"

"I couldn't do that," said Metcalf. "There wasn't anybody there."

* * *

"But my dear," protested henpecked Howard, "I've done nothing. You've been talking for an hour and a half and I haven't said a word."

"I know," replied his wife. "But you listen like a wise-guy."

9

His wife had been brooding all day and Seymour couldn't stand it. "What's wrong, sweetheart?" he asked.

"That terrible Doreen Dubin next door has a dress exactly like mine," she replied, dabbing away an angry tear.

"And I suppose you want me to buy you a new one?"

"Well," she said, "it's a lot cheaper than moving."

*　　*　　*

Did you hear about the dumb father who was taking a shower and said, "Now let me see, which pocket did I put that soap in?"

*　　*　　*

Two electrical repairmen were working on a house circuit.

"Ben," one of them said, "see those two wires?"

"Sure," said Ben.

"Good. Now just grab one of them."

Ben grabbed one of the wires. "Feel anything?" asked his partner.

"Not a thing," answered Ben.

"Good," said his partner. "Don't touch the other one or you'll drop dead."

Wife: Would you sooner lose your life
              or your money?
Husband: My life, of course. I'll need my
              money for my old age.

*   *   *

"The batter stuck to my pan," the wife sobbed.

"I thought you looked better today," replied the husband.

*   *   *

Did you hear about the dumb father who slammed his wife and kissed the door?

*   *   *

Mrs. Bostwick boasted, "My son Arthur is smarter even than Abraham Lincoln. Arthur could recite the Gettysburg Address when he was ten years old. Lincoln didn't say it till he was fifty!"

*   *   *

"Can I go outside and watch the solar eclipse?" asked Rupert.

"Okay," replied his mother, "but don't stand too close."

The motorcycle cop frantically waved the motorist over to the curb. "Your wife," said the policeman breathlessly, "fell out of your car at the last turn."

"Thank goodness it's only that," replied the motorist. "I thought I'd suddenly gone stone deaf."

"Do you always sleep between two plain sheets in summer?"

"No, I sleep between the window and the door."

*　　*　　*

"You there in the back of the room, what was the date of the signing of the Magna Carta?"

"I dunno."

"You don't know! Well, what were the dates of the Third Crusade?"

"I dunno."

"Indeed? I assigned this work last Friday. What were you doing last night?"

"I was out to a party with some friends. Didn't get home until 5 A.M."

"And you have the audacity to stand there and tell me that! Just how do you expect to pass this course?"

"I dunno, mister. You see, I just come in to fix the radiator."

*　　*　　*

Cantrell was helping sonny with his lessons. "Daddy," said the boy, "I read in school that animals have a new fur coat every winter."

"Be quiet!" said his father. "Your mother's in the next room!"

"What are you reading?" demanded the mother of her seven-year-old.

"A story about a cow jumping over the moon," was the reply.

"Throw that book away at once," commanded the mother. "How often have I told you you're too young to read science fiction?"

*   *   *

There was a severe epidemic in town so the doctor, in true medical tradition, worked around the clock by converting his kitchen into a temporary surgery. But the crowds pouring into the place made it inadequate. "Some of you will have to be vaccinated in the basement," he said.

The town socialite stood up and protested, "I, sir, will be vaccinated in the arm or not at all!"

*   *   *

Mr. and Mrs. Graham were riding on a train for the first time. They brought bananas for lunch. Just as the husband bit into his banana, the train entered a tunnel. "Did you take a bite of your banana?" he asked his wife.

"No."

"Well, don't!" replied Graham. "I did, and went blind!"

15

Tall, talented TV actor Ron Fineberg tells this turnabout twister:

Farmer Foster and his missus went to a fair. He was fascinated by the airplane rides, but he balked at the $10 tickets.

"Tell you what," said the pilot. "If you and your wife can ride without making a single sound, I won't charge you anything. Otherwise you pay the $10."

"You got yourself a deal," said Foster.

So up they went. When they got back, the pilot said, "If I hadn't been there, I never would have believed it. You never made a sound!"

"It wasn't easy, either," said the farmer. "I almost yelled when my wife fell out!"

* * *

FAMILY FUNNY FARM

A famous child psychologist addressed a women's club recently in Cleveland. During the question and answer period that followed the lecture, one lady asked, "Doctor, what do you find is the principal complaint of children today?"

"Parents," answered the psychologist.

*   *   *

Did you hear about the wife who shot her husband with a bow and arrow because she didn't want to wake the children?

Husband:	Where's yesterday's newspaper?
Wife:	I wrapped the garbage in it.
Husband:	Oh, I wanted to see it.
Wife:	There wasn't much to see . . . just some orange peels and coffee grounds.

*　　*　　*

Roland came home from the office and found his wife Selma sobbing convulsively. "I feel terrible," she told him. "I was pressing your suit and I burned a big hole right in the seat of your trousers."

"Forget it," consoled Roland. "Remember that I've got an extra pair of pants for that suit."

"Yes, and it's lucky you have," said Selma, drying her eyes. "I used them to patch the hole."

*　　*　　*

Rosalie was visiting her bandaged husband in a hospital. On the way out, she said to the nurse, "My husband always says, 'Why should I be the first to dim my headlights?' "

Father: Why are you so upset?
Mother: The garage charged me $50 for towing my car a mile. I got my money's worth though. I kept my brakes on!

* * *

Mavis Palmer, the lovely Hollywood actress, brought this beaut back from Jolly Old England:

After a hard day, Chauncey crawled into bed. He was just dropping off to sleep when his wife said, "Chauncey, close the window. It's cold outside."

"Oh, go to sleep," he said, "and you won't feel so cold."

"Close the window, Chauncey, please." insisted his wife. "It's so cold outside."

So finally he got up and slammed the window down and jumped back in bed.

"Now," he snarled at his wife, "is it warmer outside?"

* * *

Jack came home one night very late. As he was tiptoeing into the bedroom his wife called out, "Is that you, Jack?"

Jack answered rather grimly, "It damn well better be!"

A motorist following a tail light in a dense fog crashed into the car ahead of him when it stopped suddenly. "Why didn't you let me know you were going to stop?" he yelled.

"Why should I?" came a voice out of the fog. "I'm in my own garage!"

*　　*　　*

The husband of a woman who had recently learned to drive was dismayed, upon returning home, to see the car in the living room.

"How in the world did you land our car in here?" he asked.

"Nothing to it," she replied. "When I got to the kitchen, I simply made a left turn."

*　　*　　*

The middle-aged man was shuffling along, bent over at the waist, as his wife helped him into the doctor's waiting room. A woman in the office viewed the scene with sympathy.

"Arthritis with complications?" she asked.

The wife shook her head. "Do-it-yourself," she explained, "with concrete blocks."

Mrs. Brown shook her husband awake. "Will you help me straighten up the house?" she asked.

"Why?" her husband replied. "Is it tilted?"

*   *   *

A crystal-gazer informed a male customer, "I see a buried treasure."

"I know," nodded the customer wearily. "My wife's first husband."

*   *   *

Rusty Stein, the beautiful and brainy Brentwood real estate ballyhooer, brightened up the Hollywood Bowl one night with this bauble:

Mrs. Maxwell, still wearing her apron, came rushing out of the house and ran smack into her husband who was mowing the lawn.

"Going somewhere?" he asked.

"Yes. I'm baking a cake from a recipe I heard on the radio. It said to put all the ingredients in a bowl and then beat it for five minutes. Sounds silly, but I'm on my way!"

Paul had poor luck fishing. On his way home, he entered Cimoli's fish market and said to the owner, "Just stand over there and throw me five of your biggest trout."

"Throw 'em?" asked Cimoli. "What for?

"So," explained Paul, "I can tell my wife I caught 'em. I may be a poor fisherman, but I'm no liar."

A beautiful but slightly discombobulated young woman stormed into police headquarters to inquire, "Where do I apologize for shooting my husband?"

* * *

Mother: You shouldn't be swimming on a full stomach.
Father: Okay, I'll swim on my back.

* * *

"Darling," said the wife, "I really managed to save something this month! I put a hundred dollars in the bank."

"Wonderful!" replied her husband. "It wasn't so hard, was it?"

"It was easy," explained the wife. "I just tore up the bills."

* * *

Wife: Scientists claim that the average person speaks 10,000 words a day.
Husband: Yes, dear, but remember, you are far above average.

"Hey," whispered Mrs. Slough to her husband as they entered the theater, "look who they've got tonight. My favorite actor —Nosmo King." She pointed to an electric sign.

"Darling," said Mr. Slough, "that sign says 'No Smoking.'"

*　*　*

Father: Don't you think our son gets all his brains from me?

Mother: Probably. I still have all mine.

*　*　*

Lillian's parents were having their nightly squabble. "Woman," shouted the father, "you're so dumb you think Barnum and Bailey are married to each other!"

"What difference does it make," said the mother, "as long as they love each other?"

*　*　*

Potter was painting his house one hot August day. "Why are you wearing two jackets?" asked his wife.

"Because," he said, "the directions on the can say to put on two coats!"

Mr. Stone came home with a framed picture under his arm.

"Hey, what have you got there?" asked his wife, excitedly.

"I don't know much about art," replied Stone, "but I just bought an original Rembrandt for $500. It's one of the few he ever did in ballpoint!"

*　　*　　*

Mr. and Mrs. Bromwell were sitting in the living room watching television.

"Say," said the mother, "do you think Natalie Wood is her real name?"

The father thought for a minute and then replied, "Do I think whose real name is Natalie Wood?"

*　　*　　*

The father-to-be was nervously pacing up and down the hospital corridors. Finally, the nurse stopped him.

"Congratulations," she said. "You have twins."

"Wonderful," said the new father, "but please don't tell my wife—I want to surprise her."

Wife:	Darling, you know that cake you asked me to bake for you? Well, the dog ate it.
Husband:	That's okay, dear; don't cry. I'll buy you another dog!

* * *

John Searock, the Los Angeles bank exec, brandished this bit of banter:

Cliff and his wife were watching an old Gene Autry movie on TV. As Gene rode through a pass, Cliff said, "I'll bet you a dollar his horse steps in a gopher hole and falls!"

"Okay," said his wife. "You're on!"

Sure enough, the horse stumbled. After the bet was paid, Cliff said, "I ought to tell you, I saw the movie before. That's how I knew."

"So did I," said his wife, "but I didn't think a horse would be dumb enough to fall in the same hole twice!"

* * *

Husband:	Where did you get that new hat?
Wife:	Don't worry, dear. It didn't cost a thing. It was marked down from $20 to $10. So, I bought it with the $10 I saved!

27

Sam Pasternak, Kansas City record king, tells about Winslow being interviewed for a job at a detective agency.

The personnel manager asked him, "How many states are there?"

"Fifty," answered Winslow.

"Good. Now, who is the President of the United States?"

"Jimmy Carter."

"Excellent. Now, who killed Abraham Lincoln?"

"I don't know."

"Well, go find out!"

Winslow went home and his wife asked, "Did you get the job?"

"I guess so," he replied, "I'm on my first murder case."

"Say," commented Caroline to her husband, "did you know it took Michelangelo more than twenty years to paint the dome of the Sistine Chapel?"

"Yeah," said Jeffery. "But he would have done it a lot faster if he'd got himself a paint roller!"

*　*　*

Haskell rushed down to the beach where his daughter had just been rescued from drowning.

"Sir," said the handsome lifeguard, "I've just resuscitated her!"

"Then," said the father, "you're going to have to marry her!"

*　*　*

A small town decided to buy a new fire truck. When the city council met, they got into a discussion about what to do with the old one.

"I think," said Johnson, father of four, "that we should keep the old fire truck and use it for false alarms."

"I hate to say it, darling, but this toast is really tough."

"You're eating the paper plate, dear!"

*   *   *

Monroe made a lot of money on the stock market and decided to have his entire house redecorated. Mrs. Monroe insisted on helping.

When the stained glass windows were delivered, she told the contractor, "You take these right out and have all the stains removed!"

*   *   *

"Say, Harold, are you awake? There's a burglar downstairs!"

"No, I'm asleep!"

*   *   *

Pritchard walked into his living room flashing a large shiny pinkie ring.

"Hey," said his wife, "that's some diamond you got there. Is it real?"

"If it ain't," said Pritchard, "I've been cheated out of five bucks!"

MOM AND POP AT SCHOOL

In olden days, when parents carved their initials in classroom desks, they also answered test questions at which Smart Kids can now laugh. Here are some classic exam boners mama and papa were guilty of when they attended the little red school-house:

* * *

A buttress is a female butter-maker.

To germinate is becoming a naturalized German.

*　　*　　*

An optimist is a doctor who looks after your eyes. A pessimist is one who attends to your feet.

*　　*　　*

Milton was a blind poet who wrote *Paradise Lost*. When his wife died, he wrote *Paradise Regained*.

*　　*　　*

The laws of the United States do not allow a man but one wife. This is called Monotony.

*　　*　　*

Woman is the animal which possesses the greatest attachment for man.

*　　*　　*

Elizabeth was the virgin queen of England. She was very successful as a queen.

During the Napoleonic Era the crowned heads of Europe were trembling in their shoes.

*   *   *

King Henry III of England had a large abbess on his knee, which made walking difficult.

*   *   *

The American government finally decided to put all the Indians in reservoirs.

*   *   *

Seats of Congressmen are vaccinated every two years.

*   *   *

In the seventeenth century traveling was very romantic, as they had no roads, only bridal paths.

*   *   *

The Mason-Dixie Line divides the country into Mason to the north and Dixie to the south.

During the age of chivalry the knights lived in manures and had many manurial rights.

* * *

Beowulf suckled Uncle Remus and his brother who founded Rome.

* * *

Cleopatra died when an ass bit her.

* * *

One of the rights people enjoy under the Constitution is the right to keep bare arms.

* * *

A noted foreigner assisting the American colonies during the Revolution was God.

* * *

A papal bull was a ferocious bull kept by the Popes to trample on Protestants.

* * *

A polygon is a heathen who has many wives.

The American Indians traveled in canoes of birchbark on little streams that they would make themselves.

36

If a person faints in church, put her head between the knees of the nearest doctor.

* * *

The Romans worshipped a chief god called Jupiter, a goddess of love called Venice, a ruler of the underworld called Plutarch and a god of boundaries called Termite.

* * *

Mercury was the god of the weather because he is found in thermometers.

* * *

The Romans prosecuted the early Christians because they disapproved of gladiola fights and would not burn insects before the statue of the emperor.

* * *

The three chief races of men are sprints, hurdles, and long distance.

* * *

The Thirteenth Amendment to the Constitution abolished the Negroes.

The centaurs were half hoarse because they had to live in damp caves.

* * *

To keep in good health, inhale and exhale once a day, and do gymnastics.

* * *

Respiration means breathing. It is composed of aspiration and expectoration.

* * *

Air that contains more than 100 percent carbolic acid is harmful to our health.

* * *

To keep in good health, you must eat two or three vitamins every day.

* * *

The bones of the head are a frontal, two sideals, one topal and a backal.

* * *

A stethoscope is a spyglass for looking into people's chests with your ears.

A psychiatrist is a doctor with mental disorders.

*   *   *

A skeleton is a man with his outside off and his inside sticking out.

*   *   *

Gender is how you tell that a man is masculine, feminine, or neuter.

*   *   *

Reproduction is the process by which an organist is able to produce others of its kind.

*   *   *

Puerility is the state of being pure, like virginity.

*   *   *

They carried Geiger counters to map out the cosmetic rays which are fatal to man.

The chief cause of divorce is marriage.

* * *

Bigotry is having two wives at the same time.

* * *

Trigonometry is when a man marries three wives at the same time.

* * *

The Single Tax is a tax on bachelors.

* * *

A Senator is front-half man and back-half horse.

* * *

A mayor is a female horse.

* * *

An apiary is a house you keep apes in.

Average is a nest. Hens lay on the average.

* * *

The elegant repast was topped off by a delicious frozen mouse.

* * *

Many rocks contain the fossil footprints of fishes.

* * *

The dodo was a bird the size of a pigeon that is wholly distinguished now.

* * *

In order to keep milk from turning sour, it should be kept in the cow.

* * *

The cow furnishes milk. A calf is a young cow who furnishes jelly.

A mammal is an animal that succors its ancestors.

*   *   *

Centipedes are animals found by the hundreds, while millipedes are found by the millions.

*   *   *

All mammals have memory glands.

*   *   *

What are six animals peculiar to the Arctic region?
Six polar bears.

*   *   *

The Equator is a menagerie lion running around the earth.

*   *   *

The Black Hole of Calcutta had only one small widow, and more than a hundred Englishmen died when they were shut up there for the night.

The climate of Bombay is such that its natives have to live in other places.

*　　*　　*

The Red Sea and the Mediterranean Sea are connected by the Sewage Canal.

*　　*　　*

Arabia gave us the dismal system, which we still use in counting.

*　　*　　*

The international date line is in the middle of the Pacific Ocean. It is the cause of day and night.

*　　*　　*

The moon is more important than the sun, because it shines at night when it is needed.

*　　*　　*

Dust is mud with the juice squeezed out.

44

Two famous Shakespearean plays: *Romeo* and *Juliet*.

*   *   *

A hamlet is an English dish consisting of ham and eggs cooked together.

*   *   *

KNOCK KNOCKS

During Prohibition (1919 to 1933) the speakeasy became the popular underground hangout.

In order to gain entrance to these "gin mills," you had to knock on the door twice and use a password like, "Joe sent me." This led to a gag form that kids of all ages get a kick out of still.

Here's a sample:

KNOCK KNOCK ...

Who's there?
Irving.
Irving, who?
Irving a good time, wish you were here.

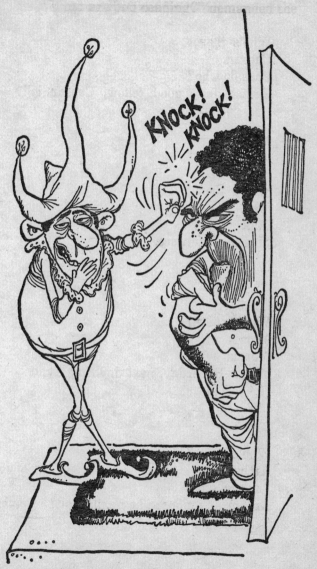

47

KNOCK KNOCK...

Who's there?
Caesar.
Caesar, who?
Caesar Jolly good fellow, Caesar jolly
   good fellow.

* * *

Who's there?
Max.
Max, who?
Max no difference.

* * *

Who's there?
Morris.
Morris, who?
Morris Saturday, next day Sunday.

* * *

Who's there?
Arthur.
Arthur, who?
Arthur any more at home like you?

KNOCK KNOCK ...

Who's there?
Felix.
Felix, who?
Felix cited.

* * *

Who's there?
Checker.
Checker, who?
Check her yourself, she's not my type.

* * *

Who's there?
Amos.
Amos, who?
A mosquito.

* * *

Who's there?
Luke.
Luke, who?
Luke and see.

KNOCK KNOCK . . .

Who's there?
Boo Boo.
Boo Boo, who?
Don't cry.

*   *   *

Who's there?
Yukon.
Yukon, who?
Yukon have it, I don't want it.

*   *   *

Who's there?
Sofa.
Sofa, who?
Sofa, so good.

*   *   *

Who's there?
Texas.
Texas, who?
Texas two a long time to get together.

Who's there?
Welfare.
Welfare, who?
Welfare crying out loud, look who's
    here!

* * *

Who's there?
Icepick.
Icepick, who?
Icepick for the people of New York.

* * *

Who's there?
Eiffel.
Eiffel, who?
Eiffel down and hurt myself.

* * *

Who's there?
Hugh.
Hugh, who?
Yoo-hoo, yourself.

KNOCK KNOCK ...

Who's there?
Butcher.
Butcher, who?
Butcher arms around me honey, hold
    me tight.

*   *   *

Who's there?
Welcome.
Welcome, who?
Welcome up and see me some time.

*   *   *

Who's there?
Celeste.
Celeste, who?
Celeste time I'm going to ask you.

*   *   *

Who's there?
Chester.
Chester, who?
Chester minute and I'll see.

KNOCK KNOCK ...

Who's there?
Dwayne.
Dwayne, who?
Dwayne the bathtub, I'm dwowning.

* * *

Who's there?
Madame.
Madame, who?
Ma dam foot is caught in your door.

* * *

Who's there?
Allison.
Allison, who?
Allison Wonderland.

* * *

Who's there?
Hiawatha.
Hiawatha, who?
Hiawatha good girl until I met you.

Who's there?
Banana.
Banana who?
Knock knock.
Who's there?
Banana.
Banana who?
Knock knock.
Who's there?
Orange.
Orange who?
Orange you glad I didn't say banana
    again?

*   *   *

Who's there?
Windy.
Windy who?
Windy moon comes over the mountain.

*   *   *

Who's there?
Minerva.
Minerva who?
Minerva's wreck from all these Knock
    Knocks.

LITTLE WILLIES

In humor history there have been many joke crazes. Elephant jokes, good news, bad news, etc. During the sixties, sick jokes became the fad. Gags like:

"Other than that, Mrs. Lincoln, how was the show?"

*   *   *

"Can Bobby come out and play baseball with us? We want to use his wooden leg as a bat!"

In the gas chamber just before the execution, the chaplain said to the criminal, "Is there anything I can do for you as a last request?"

"Yes," replied the criminal, "hold my hand."

* * *

The first recorded sick jokes were done over a hundred years ago and took the form of four-line poems known as "Little Willies." Here is a short collection of those early sickies:

Little Willie, in bows and sashes,
Fell in the fire and got burned to ashes.
In the winter, when the weather was chilly,
No one liked to poke up Willie.

* * *

Little Willie hung his sister;
She was dead before we missed her.
"Willie's always up to tricks
Ain't he cute? He's only six!"

Willie, with a thirst for gore,
Nailed the baby to the door.
Mother said, with humor quaint,
"Willie, dear, don't spoil the paint."

* * *

Willie saw some dynamite,
Couldn't understand it quite.
Curiosity never pays;
It rained Willie seven days.

* * *

Willie in the cauldron fell;
See the grief on mother's brow!
Mother loved her darling well
Darling's quite hard-boiled by now.

* * *

Making toast at the fireside
Nurse fell in the fire and died;
And, what makes it ten times worse
All the toast was burned with nurse.

An angel bore dear Uncle Joe
To rest beyond the stars.
I miss him, oh! I miss him so—
He had such good cigars!

* * *

Willie fell down the elevator
Wasn't found till six days later.
Then the neighbors sniffed, "Gee Whiz!
What a spoiled child Willie is!"

* * *

Into the family drinking well
Willie pushed his sister Nell.
She's there yet—the water kilt her,
And we have to use a filter.

* * *

Little Willie, full of glee,
Put radium in Grandma's tea.
Now he thinks it quite a lark
To see her shining in the dark.

Willie, in a fit insane,
Thrust his head beneath a train.
All were quite surprised to find
How it broadened Willie's mind.

* * *

Willie on the railroad track—
The engine gave a squeal.
The engineer just took a spade
And scraped him off the wheel.

* * *

Willie with his little shears
Clipped off baby brother's ears.
This made baby so unsightly,
Mother raised her eyebrows slightly.

* * *

Little Willie, mean as hell,
Pushed his sister in the well.
Mother said while drawing water,
"My, it's hard to raise a daughter."

Willie's cute as cute can be!
Beneath his brother, only three,
He lit a stick of dynamite.
Now Bubby's simply out of sight!

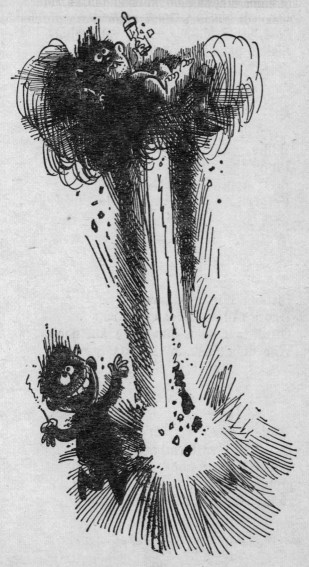

Willie, who is such a droop,
Put arsenic in Grandpa's soup.
"My," said Mother, "how distressing;
Sister, pass the salad dressing."

* * *

Willie, with a fearful curse,
Flung the coffee pot at nurse.
As it struck her on the nose,
Father said, "How straight he throws!"

* * *

Little Willie on a farm
Had a fall and broke his arm;
Of all that knew him there was none
Who didn't ask, "What! Only one?"

* * *

Little Will, with father's gun,
Punctured grandma, just for fun.
Mother frowned at the merry lad;
It was the last shell father had.

Willie, bored with stealing cars,
Swiped a rocket, flew to Mars.
He there pursued his normal pattern,
So now the Martians live on Saturn.

*   *   *

Little Willie, bless his britches,
Is back to put us all in stitches.
Prince of caper, jape and antic,
He's kept five generations frantic.

*   *   *

RIDDLES TO STUMP DUMB PARENTS

Why do we call our language the mother tongue?

Because father never gets a chance to use it.

*　　*　　*

What do women do with the years they take off their true ages?

Add them to the ages of their best friends.

Why do some babies' hair turn snow-white at the age of three months?

They have near-sighted mothers—who keep powdering the wrong end.

*   *   *

What did the mother say when she learned that her son had consumed 37 batter cakes at one sitting?

"How waffle!"

*   *   *

When a little boy puts his socks on wrong side out, what does his mother do?

Turns the hose on him.

*   *   *

What is the surest way for a husband to make his wife angry?

Pull the wool over her eyes with the wrong yarn.

*   *   *

When does a wife become a magician?

When she turns an old rake into a lawn mower.

Why are children like flannel?
Because they shrink from washing.

*   *   *

What is the hardest thing about learning to ride a bicycle?
The pavement.

*   *   *

Why are promises like fat ladies who faint in church?
Because the sooner they are carried out, the better.

*   *   *

Two Indians are standing on a hill, and one is the father of the other's son. What relation are the two Indians to each other?
Husband and wife.

*   *   *

Why does the Indian wear feathers in his hair?
To keep his wigwam.

*   *   *

Why do birds fly south?
Because it's too far to walk.

What are the three most common causes of forest fires?

Men, women, and children.

* * *

What is a perfectionist?

A father who takes infinite pains—and usually gives them to everybody around him.

* * *

When is a mother flea saddest?

When her children go to the dogs.

* * *

Why is a rabbit's nose usually shiny?

Because he has the powder puff at the wrong end.

* * *

When Baby Rabbit asks Mama Rabbit, "How did I come into the world?" what does Mama Rabbit answer?

"A magician pulled you out of a hat."

What is the difference between a bottle of medicine and a bad boy?

One is well shaken before taken, and the other should be taken and well shaken.

* * *

What is the difference between a fisherman and a lazy schoolboy?

One baits his hook, while the other hates his book.

* * *

What American has had the largest family?

George Washington, who was the "father of his country."

* * *

How can you divide nineteen apples absolutely equally between seven small boys?

Make the apples into applesauce, and measure it out very carefully.

* * *

What is the oldest piece of furniture in the world?

The multiplication table.

What animal took the most baggage into Noah's ark, and what animals the least?

The elephant took his trunk, but the fox and the rooster took only a brush and comb between them.

*   *   *

What three words, which read the same backward and forward, did Adam use when he introduced himself to Eve:

"Madam, I'm Adam."

*   *   *

How many apples were eaten in the Garden of Eden?

Eve ate, and Adam, too, and the devil won. That makes eleven in all.

*   *   *

Who was the best businesswoman in the Bible?

Pharoah's daughter. She drew a prophet from a rush on the bank.

*   *   *

When was the first tennis game played in biblical times?

When Moses served in Pharoah's court.

Who was the most popular actor in the Bible?

Samson. He brought down the house.

71

If a woman were to change her sex, what religion would she then represent?

She would be a he-then.

*   *   *

What made Francis Scott Key famous?

He knew all the verses of "The Star-Spangled Banner."

*   *   *

What do they call the cabs lined up at airports and railroad terminals?

The yellow rows of taxis.

*   *   *

What do they call a man in Texas who is six feet tall?

A midget.

*   *   *

What's the difference between a pessimist and an optimist?

A pessimist is a female who's afraid she won't be able to squeeze her car into a very small parking space. An optimist is a male who thinks she won't try.

Why did Robin Hood rob only the rich?
Because the poor had no money.

*   *   *

What's the real reason men and women
go to nudist camps?
To air their differences.

*   *   *

What happens when the human body is
submerged in water?
The telephone rings.

*   *   *

What is the best thing to put into an
ice-cream soda?
A straw.

*   *   *

Why is it that every man's trousers are
too short?
Because his legs always stick out two
feet.

Why are tall people always the laziest?
Because they are longer in bed than short people.

* * *

Why is a tailor an expert lover?
He knows how to press a suit.

* * *

What kind of horse can take several thousand people for a ride at the same time?
A race horse.

* * *

What happened to the girl who swallowed a spoon?
She couldn't stir.

* * *

What is worse than a giraffe with a sore throat?
A centipede with sore feet.

* * *

What is worse than raining cats and dogs?
Hailing taxis.

What is better than to give credit where credit is due?
Give cash.

*   *   *

If a chicken could talk, what kind of language would it speak?
Foul language.

*   *   *

What is the best way to keep fish from smelling?
Cut off their noses.

*   *   *

What has two heads, six feet, one tail and four ears?
A man on horseback.

*   *   *

What is the difference between a hill and a pill?
A hill is hard to get up, while a pill is hard to get down.

I have four legs, yet only one foot. What am I?

A bed.

* * *

Why doesn't a steam locomotive like to sit down?

Because it has a tender behind.

* * *

CHILDREN'S LIP

There will always be a generation gap between children and their parents. We all might as well get some fun out of it. Here's what some kids say:

Parents are the last people on earth who ought to have children.

* * *

Parents are all alike; first they try to get you to walk and talk, and then they try to get you to sit down and shut up.

A parent is someone who treats an adolescent like a child, yet expects him to act like an adult.

* * *

Parents are people who always think their children would behave much better if they didn't play with the brats next door.

* * *

It's very hard for rich parents not to be poor parents.

* * *

Many a mother wishes the schools would do a better job of bringing up her children.

* * *

Parents are inconsistent. First they want us home early because we're children, and later, because we're not children.

* * *

The generation that criticizes the younger generation is always the one that raised it.

Politicians who were born of poor but honest parents usually have children who were not.

* * *

Many problem children go by the name of parents.

* * *

Children are hereditary. If your parents didn't have any, chances are you won't either.

* * *

We get our parents when they are too old for us to change their habits.

* * *

I keep hoping my parents will eventually run out of advice.

* * *

My folks are sending me away to school so they won't have to help me with my homework.

I was an unwanted child—my parents
expected a Buick.

There's one thing about us children—
we never go around showing snapshots of
our grandparents.

*   *   *

My mom is very neat. She empties ash-
trays before they're used.

*   *   *

My mom talks so much, I get hoarse
listening to her.

*   *   *

My mom had a nervous breakdown trying to fit round tomatoes into square sand-
wiches.

*   *   *

My early struggles started when mother
tried to wash my ears.

*   *   *

When my mom first got married she
tried to squeeze the tomato cans in the
supermarket to see if they were fresh.

My mother can only boil eggs for five seconds. She claims if she holds them in the boiling water any longer, she burns her hand.

*   *   *

My mother is so dumb, she tried to open an egg with a can opener.

*   *   *

Whenever I think of the biscuits my mother makes, I get a lump in my throat.

*   *   *

My mama makes eggnog with hard-boiled eggs.

*   *   *

My mom is an excellent driver. She only has trouble with starting, stopping, turning and parking.

*   *   *

My mother is just learning to drive. Around the house we call her, "O-ma the Dent Maker."

Does my mom know how to drive? She just got a ticket for making a U-turn in the Lincoln Tunnel!

* * *

When two cars are double-parked, the one parked by my mother is the one on top.

* * *

My father is so henpecked he has to wash and iron his own apron.

* * *

My father has a split personality and I hate both of them.

* * *

A smart father is one who thinks twice before saying nothing.

My father told me everything about the birds and the bees. He doesn't know anything about girls.

* * *

We finally had to move from Cincinnati. My father couldn't spell it.

My father is so lazy he always runs his car over a bump just to knock the ashes off his cigar.

* * *

When I was sixteen, my dad said, "Son, I want to sit down and talk to you about the facts of life!"
I said, "Okay, Pop, what do you want to know?"

* * *

My father told me about the birds and the bees—then I told him about the booze and the broads.

* * *

My father said, "You can't go to the X-rated movie, you'll see something you shouldn't!" He was right. I saw my father in the first row.

* * *

"Once my mother and father agreed it would be helpful for each to tell the other their faults."
"How did it work?"
"They haven't spoken for five years."

Frank Bresee, the genius Golden Days of Radio creator, handed over this howler:

Miles returned to his posh Beverly Hills home from college one hot afternoon and decided to cool off with a dip in the family pool.

"Wait a minute, son," announced his father, "you can't go in the pool with long hair!"

"What?" exclaimed Miles.

"You heard me! It's unhealthy. Get a haircut and you can go in!"

"But, Dad, some of history's greatest men had long hair," said the young man.

"Those are the rules."

"Moses had long hair."

"Moses can't swim in our pool, either."

"Darling, eat your spinach. It will put color in your cheeks."

"But, mom, who wants green cheeks?"

*　　*　　*

Father: My boy, I never kissed a girl until I met your mother. Will you be able to say the same thing to your son?

Junior: Yes, Dad. But not with such a straight face.

*　　*　　*

"My father fell asleep in the bathtub with the water running."

"Did the bathtub overflow?"

"Nope. Pop sleeps with his mouth open."

*　　*　　*

His grandmother watched the boy eat his soup with the wrong spoon, grasp the utensils with the wrong fingers, eat the main course with his hands, and pour tea into the saucer and blow on it.

"Hasn't watching your mother and dad at the dinner table taught you anything?" she asked.

"Yeah," said the boy. "Never to get married."

"Here's a book: *How to Torture Your Father*."

"I don't need that. I have a system of my own."

*　　*　　*

A little girl wrote this essay:

PEOPLE

People are composed of girls and boys, also men and women.

Boys are no good until they grow up and get married.

Men who don't get married are no good either.

Girls are young women who will be ladies when they graduate.

Boys are an awful bother. They want everything they see except soap.

If I had my way, half the boys in the world would be girls, and the other half dolls.

My ma is a woman and my pa is a man. A woman is a grown-up girl with children.

My pa is such a nice man I guess he must have been a little girl when he was a little boy.

*　　*　　*

PARENT'S LIB

Mom and Dad have been taking it on the chin all through this book. Okay, kids, look out! Now it's their turn:

Every parent wishes he knew as much as his children think he does, or as much as his children think they do.

Children should be seen and not had.

* * *

Children have become so expensive that only the poor can afford them.

* * *

They say children brighten up a home. That's right—they never turn off the lights.

* * *

An allowance is what you pay your children to live with you.

* * *

Children are the light of the house . . . but when you have half a dozen, it's time to shut off the light.

* * *

How to keep your teenage daughter out of hot water:
Put some dishes in it.

If you wonder where your child left his roller skates, try walking around the house in the dark.

Babysitters say that a good way to keep a child quiet is to let him suck on a bottle of glue.

*　　*　　*

PARENTAL PROVERB

'Tis better to have loved and lost—
than to do homework for three children.

*　　*　　*

You can tell a child is growing up when he stops asking where he came from and starts refusing to tell where he is going.

*　　*　　*

Just when your children get old enough that you can stand them, they can't stand you.

*　　*　　*

My children are finally grown up. My daughter started to put on lipstick and my son started to wipe it off.

My son never comes when I call him. He'll probably grow up to be a waiter.

* * *

My kid shows signs of becoming an executive. Already he takes two hours for lunch.

* * *

My son now has a leading part in the theater. He is head usher.

* * *

I once got a dog for my son. It was the best trade I ever made.

* * *

My little daughter is so nervous, she developed an ulcerette.

* * *

My son's a fine broth of a boy. Too bad some of his noodles are missing.

Ever since he was eight years old, we've been pleading with our son to run away from home.

*　　*　　*

My child eats dry toast and washes it down with crackers.

*　　*　　*

My infant is eating solids now—keys, newspapers, pencils . . .

*　　*　　*

My daughter's in the dungarees and loafers stage. She wears dungarees and dates loafers.

*　　*　　*

My kid called her legion of boyfriends so steadily that when she finally got married the grateful telephone company retired her number.

At a child's birthday party, the hostess had this to say:

"Now remember, kids, there will be a special prize for the little boy who goes home first."

* * *

Talented TV and nightclub jester, Jeremy Vernon, says,

"I attended one wedding ceremony of two high school kids where the bridegroom wept for two hours.

"It seems the bride got a bigger piece of cake than he did."

* * *

Kids today are pretty expensive. Now I know the answer to that age-old question, "What is a home without children?" PAID FOR!

* * *

I've got a neighbor who would have been divorced years ago if it wasn't for the kids —she wouldn't take them and he wouldn't have them.

Parents, here's some good advice for you to get closer to your children.

Join them in their work, join them in their games, join in their problems, but if you can't join 'em—beat 'em!

*   *   *

Today you ask a kid to do something— forget it. I asked my kid to help his mother with the dinner dishes. He thought I was talking about a charity ball—he wanted ten bucks a plate!

*   *   *

"Do you think your boy will forget all he learned in college?"

"I hope so. He can't make a living necking."

*   *   *

"I want to take my son out of this lousy college."

"But he's at the head of his class."

"That's why I think this is a lousy college."

"What's your son going to be when he graduates?"

"An old man."

* * *

A father woke early one morning and decided to surprise the family by making oatmeal for everybody for breakfast.

He was spooning out a bowl for his four-year-old son Freddie. "Want honey on it?" the father asked.

"Yes," said Freddie.

"And milk?"

"Yes."

"Butter, too?"

"Yes."

He gave the bowl to the boy, who just stared at it and pushed it away.

"What's the matter?" his dad asked. "I put everything you wanted on it."

"I don't like oatmeal!" answered Freddie.

* * *

Did you hear about the teenage girl who has been trying to run away from home for a year, but every time she gets to the front door the phone rings?

A mother, annoyed because her fifteen-year-old daughter had been calling her boyfriend too frequently, took a tip from a former wartime advertisement and posted a sign over the telephone: "Is this call necessary?"

Next day there appeared, penciled on the card, "How can I tell till I've made it?"

*   *   *

Doris, the most talkative teenager in her neighborhood, was burning up the wire one evening on the downstairs telephone, much to the fuming irritation of her father. Finally, after fifteen minutes of the nonsensical conversation between daughter and No. 1 girl friend, he broke in.

"Doris," he stormed, "I'd like to use the phone. Why in heaven's name don't you use your private phone—the one I got you for Christmas?"

"Gee, Dad, don't be a square," said Doris. "Someone might call me on my phone."

*   *   *

Mr. Waters: What's your son's average income?

Mr. Hardy: Between 3 and 4 A.M.

100

"Doctor," said the pale-faced man to his physician, "I'm in an awful state! Whenever the phone rings, I almost jump out of my skin. The doorbell gives me the shakes. If I see a stranger at the door, I start trembling. I'm even afraid to look at a newspaper. What's come over me, anyway?"

"There, there," said the M.D. "I know what you're going through. My teenage daughter just learned to drive, too."

*   *   *

A mother discovered her little daughter fighting with the boy next door. After parting them, she lectured her daughter.

"Next time," she said, "I don't want you hitting Johnny back. Remember you're a lady. Out-talk him!"

*   *   *

Mother: Ethel, Kirk brought you home very late last night.
Ethel: Yes, it was late, Mother. Did the noise disturb you?
Mother: No dear, it wasn't the noise. It was the silence.

The teenage girl, after two lessons from the driving school, took her father out for a spin in the family car. "Oh, Daddy!" she trilled. "Doesn't speeding over hill and dale make you glad you're still alive?"

"Glad? I'm amazed!"

Mother: Now, Junior, be a good boy and say "Ah-h-h," so the doctor can get his finger out of your mouth.

* * *

For weeks Horace had been praising his new girl friend, until his parents felt they should invite the girl to the house for dinner.

The next day Horace's father asked him to reiterate his feelings about the girl. "She is all the world to me, father," said the boy.

"Then, son," said the father, "you'd better see more of the world."

* * *

Father: What's the matter with Fritz?
Mother: He just dug a hole, and now he wants to bring it into the house.

Children are a great comfort in your old age—and they help you reach it faster.

* * *

Vince Scully, the brilliant Los Angeles Dodgers' play-by-play broadcaster, told this beaut one night during a break in the action:

It was the last day of school. A mother walked into her son's room and shouted, "Come on, Alvin, get up! It's time to go to school!"

Alvin pulled the sheets over his head and said, "No! I'm not going! I hate school! I'm sick of school! Sick of it!"

"But, sonny, you have to go!"

"Give me three good reasons why I should go!"

"Well, first of all, you are the principal. . . ."

* * *

As a child, I was the type of a kid my mother told me not to play with.

"From the day your baby is born," counseled a famous scholar, "you must teach him to do without things. Children today love luxury too much. They have execrable manners, flout authority, have no respect for their elders. They no longer rise when their parents or teachers enter the room. What kind of awful creatures will they be when they grow up?"

The scholar who wrote these words, incidentally, was Socrates, shortly before his death in 399 B.C.

*   *   *

All KIDding Aside . . .

Like it's obvious, parents are the "pits." They think just because you live in *their* house, eat *their* food, and wear the clothes *they* buy for you that they can boss you around all the time! But they have another think coming. They may think we think that they're OK . . . but what do *we* really think?

Well, here's our side of the story, and doesn't it all sound like home, sweet home. If the generation gap has got you, or if you're the proud owner of a late model D.P. (Dumb Parent), the following pages ought to be good for a short escape.

It might also be fun to cut out a few appropriate jokes and put them in the old man's wallet, paste 'em on a mirror in the bathroom, or mail 'em on an anonymous postcard.

Books by Larry Wilde

The Official Polish/Italian Joke Book
The Official Jewish/Irish Joke Book
The Official Virgins/Sex Maniacs Joke Book
The Official Black Folks/White Folks Joke Book
MORE The Official Polish/Italian Joke Book
MORE The Official Jewish/Irish Joke Book
The Official Democrat/Republican Joke Book
The Official Religious/NOT SO Religious Joke Book
The Official Smart Kids/Dumb Parents Joke Book
The Official Golfers Joke Book
The LAST Official Polish Joke Book
The Official Dirty Joke Book
The Official Cat Lovers/Dog Lovers Joke Book
The LAST Official Italian Joke Book
　　and
The 1979 Official Ethnic Calendar
　　also
The Complete Book of Ethnic Humor (Corwin Books)
How The Great Comedy Writers Create Laughter
　(Nelson-Hall)
The Great Comedians (Citadel Press)

THE OFFICIAL SMART KIDS JOKE BOOK

by Larry Wilde

PINNACLE BOOKS   LOS ANGELES

THE OFFICIAL SMART KIDS/DUMB PARENTS
JOKE BOOK

Text Copyright © 1977 by Larry Wilde
Illustrations Copyright © 1977 by Pinnacle Books, Inc.

An original Pinnacle Books edition, published for the
first time anywhere.

ISBN: 0-523-40468-9

First printing, March 1977
Second printing, September 1977
Third printing, November 1977
Fourth printing, May 1978
Fifth printing, August 1978
Sixth printing, May 1979
Seventh printing, July 1979

Cover illustration by Ron Wing

Printed in the United States of America

PINNACLE BOOKS, INC.
2029 Century Park East
Los Angeles, California 90067

This book is dedicated to
brothers Milt and Ben and sister Mimi—
The smartest kids on Oak Street

ABOUT THE AUTHOR

This eighth "Official" joke book represents a milestone in the unusually versatile career of Larry Wilde. With his book sales over 2,500,000, Wilde is now the architect of the largest selling humor series in the history of publishing.

Comedian Larry Wilde has entertained at America's leading hotels and nightclubs, while *actor* Larry Wilde is frequently seen on television commercials and on many of the situation comedy series (Mary Tyler Moore, Sanford and Son, and the like).

Born in Jersey City, New Jersey, Wilde served two years in the United States Marine Corps and has a bachelor's degree from the University of Miami, Florida.

Besides the Pinnacle joke book series, *author* Larry Wilde has penned articles for professional journals as well as *Gallery, Genesis, TV Guide, Penthouse, Coronet, Cosmo Forum,* and other popular magazines.

He is also the author of two serious works dealing with comedy technique: *The Great Comedians* (Citadel) and *How the Great Comedy Writers Create Laughter* (Nelson-Hall).

Larry is married to the former Maryruth Poulos and lives in Los Angeles where, between Las Vegas engagements and concert performances, as *lecturer* Larry Wilde, he delivers talks on humor. In addition, Wilde conducts a class in comedy at UCLA, where he is referred to on campus as *Professor* Larry Wilde.

CONTENTS

THE OFFICIAL
SMART KIDS
JOKE BOOK

FROM THE MOUTHS OF BABES

Four-year-old Cindy was alone in the nursery one evening when her brother Kevin, three, knocked on the door. "Hey, let me in," said the boy.

"I can't let you in," said Cindy. "I'm in my nightgown and Mommy says it isn't right for little boys to see little girls in their nightgowns."

Kevin thought about this for a minute and was about to walk away when his sister called from inside the door.

"You can come in now. I took it off."

1

Photographer: See the birdie?

Bright Child: Mister, just pay attention to your exposure, focal length, distance, and lighting so you won't ruin the plate.

* * *

"Young man, there were two cookies in the pantry this morning. May I ask how it happens that there is only one now?"

"Must have been so dark I didn't see the other one."

* * *

Two small girls were playing together one afternoon in the park.

"I wonder what time it is," said one of them.

"Well, it can't be four o'clock yet," replied the other, "because my mother said I was to be home at four, and I'm not."

* * *

"When I grow up," bragged four-year-old Flora, "I'm going to be a Brownie."

"So what?" declared Albert, her three-year-old neighbor. "I'm going to be a bologna sandwich."

2

Ingrid Davis, the lovely Miami socialite, tells about the kindly old lady who stopped a toddler on Lincoln Road and asked, "What's your name?"

"Morris," answered the boy.

"Morris what?" persisted the senior citizen. "What's your last name?"

"My last name?" pondered the little guy. "Oh, I know. Morris Stop That Immediately."

* * *

"Why do you want to be a bird?" asked the father of his six-year-old son.

"Because you can fly anywhere you want to, and you never have to stop, not even to go to the bathroom."

* * *

Pat Patterson, whose husband Dick is one of television's brightest comedy stars, tells this titillator:

An usher patroling the seats of the local movie theater came across a small boy sitting calmly watching the picture.

"Hey, you," said the usher, tapping the youngster on the shoulder. "How come you're not in school?"

"Oh, it's okay," said the boy. "I've got chicken pox."

3

A six-year-old ran up and down the supermarket aisles shouting frantically, "Marian! Marian!"

Finally reunited with his mother, he was chided by her, "You shouldn't call me 'Marian.' I'm your mother, you know."

"I know," he replied, "but the store is full of mothers."

Peter: What's an adult?
Marge: Someone who has stopped growing
except in the middle.

*   *   *

A boy's uncle was surprised to find him
home and said, "I thought you were in
school. Are you all right?"

"I'm fine," said the boy. "I'm sick."

*   *   *

Lady: Oh, isn't he sweet. Little boy,
if you give me a kiss, I'll give
you a bright new penny.
Little Boy: I get twice as much at home
for just taking castor oil.

*   *   *

"Mommie?" whimpered the cute little
youngster. "Do you love me?"

"Yes, darling."

"Then why not divorce daddy and marry
the man in the candy store?"

*   *   *

Benjie: Mom, do you remember that vase
you always worried I would break?
Mom: Yes, what about it?
Benjie: Your worries are over.

A small girl boarded a streetcar in Boston and the conductor asked kindly, "How old are you, little girl?"

"If the corporation doesn't object," sniffed the tot, "I'd prefer to pay full fare and keep my statistics to myself."

* * *

Tom Ireland, the sprightly retired Los Angeles Shell Oil exec, loves this lulu:

The inquisitive little four-year-old sat on grandpa's lap and played with his gold watch chain.

"When I die," cooed loving gramp, "this gold chain will go to you."

"It's pretty," nodded the little darling. "When are you going to die?"

* * *

Hostess   (at a children's birthday party): Jackie does your mother allow you to have two pieces of cake when you are at home?

Jackie   (who had just asked for a second piece): No, ma'am.

Hostess: Well, do you think she'd like you to have two pieces here?

Jackie: Oh, she wouldn't care. This isn't her cake!

The stern-faced middle-aged woman said to a little boy, "Sonny, does your mother know you smoke?"

"Does your husband know you stop and talk to strange men on the street?" replied the youngster.

"There you go tracking mud all over the house. Didn't I tell you to wipe your feet before you came in?"

"Oh, nobody's blaming you, mom. You did all you could."

* * *

Mother took a good look at Sally. "Oh, my!" she said. "What did you do?"

"I fell in the mud," said Sally.

"Oh, Sally," said her mother. "With your good dress on?"

"Well," she replied, "I didn't have time to take it off!"

* * *

A six-year-old came home with a new ball.

"Where did you get that?" asked his mother.

"George gave it to me for doing him a favor," replied the boy. "I was hitting him on the back and he asked me to stop."

* * *

A little boy went to the ballet for the first time with his father and watched the girls dance around on their toes for a while.

Then he asked, "Why don't they just get taller girls?"

Two young brothers were whispering at the kitchen door as they hungrily eyed the freshly baked cake mother had made.

"You ask her if we can have some now," said the seven-year-old.

"No, you'd better," said the five-year-old. "You've known her longer than I have!"

*　　*　　*

Jay Stewart, the lovable "Let's Make a Deal" announcer, came up with this cutie:

Jimmy had returned home from a party and his mother, knowing his weakness, looked him straight in the eye and asked, "Are you sure you didn't ask Mrs. Smith for a second piece of cake?"

"No, mother," replied Jimmy. "I only asked for the recipe, so that you could make one like it, and she gave me two more pieces on her own."

*　　*　　*

A lady decided to have the little neighbor boy stay for lunch one day. As he began eating she watched him struggling to manipulate his knife and fork.

Hoping to be helpful, she said, "Are you sure you can cut your steak?"

"Oh, yes," he replied. "We often have it this tough at home."

Dale Marsh, the handsome Hancock Park bank exec, suggested this howler:

Cathy, aged five, and her playmate neighbor Bobby, aged four, often played husband and wife. One day the "married" couple stopped at the home of Widow Wallace.

"Hi," said Cathy when the door was opened, "my husband and I stopped by to say hello."

"Fine," said the widow, going along with the moppets. "Won't you come in and have some cookies and lemonade?"

An hour later the children had consumed a dozen cookies and over a quart of lemonade. Finally the little girl stood up and said, "I think we had better go now."

"Why not have some more lemonade?" asked Mrs. Wallace.

"No, I think we'd better go," said Cathy. "My husband just wet his pants."

Mother: Robby, did you thank Mrs. Green for the party?

Robby: I was going to, but a girl ahead of me said "Thank you," and Mrs. Green told her not to mention it. So I didn't.

*   *   *

Little Max ran by a policeman on the block at top speed. Five minutes later he rushed by again as fast as the first time.

After several trips, the policeman stopped him. "What's the idea, sonny?" he asked. "What's the rush?"

Max looked up and shouted, "I am running away from home!"

"Oh," said the officer. "But you've gone around this same block at least five times."

"I know it!" shouted the boy as he started running again. "My mother won't let me cross the street."

*   *   *

A man heard his wife tell their six-year-old to be nice to daddy because Father's Day was coming.

"You know what Father's Day is, don't you, dear?" she asked.

"Of course," replied the kid. "It's just like Mother's Day only you don't have to spend as much on the present."

Girl:	Grandfather, make like a frog.
Grandpa:	What do you mean, make like a frog?
Girl:	Mommy says we're going to make a lot of money when you croak!

*   *   *

Conrad was six years old and had never spoken a word. His parents spent a small fortune taking him to a psychiatrist, but it didn't help.

Finally at the dinner table one evening he looked down at his plate of food and said, "Take this slop away; it's terrible!"

His parents were elated and wept with joy. "You can talk!" cried his mother. "How come you've never spoken before this?"

"Up to now," said Conrad, "everything has been okay."

*   *   *

Barber:	Well, son, how would you like your hair cut?
Sonny:	Just like dad's, and be sure to leave that little round hole on the top where his head comes through.

After little Lori had a tussle with a neighborhood friend, the girl's mother scolded her. "Remember, Lori," said the mother, "that it was the devil who suggested to you that you pull little Alice's hair."

"I suppose so," said Lori. "But kicking her in the shin was my own idea."

*   *   *

"So what's new at your house?" a nosy neighbor asked of little Frankie.

"Who knows?" answered the little fellow. "They spell everything!"

*   *   *

Gloria was an extremely well-endowed young lady, so she was taking a chance in wearing a bikini.

One day, while walking along the beach, she bent over to pick up a shell and the top of her bikini split and fell off.

Gloria quickly threw her arms across her chest and rushed into the water.

A six-year-old boy who had noticed Gloria heading for the surf, shouted, "Hey, lady, if you are going to drown those puppies, I'll take the one with the pink nose."

16

Millie Ginsberg, the Chicago housewife tennis champ, relates this incident between son Mark and husband Jack:

"Didn't you promise me to be a good boy?"

"Yes, father."

"And didn't I promise you no spending money if you weren't?"

"Yes, father. But since I've broken my promise, you sure don't have to keep yours."

*   *   *

A proud father introduced his son for the first time at the office. "How old are you, sonny?" asked his dad's co-worker.

"When I'm home I'm seven," said the child, "and when I'm on a bus I'm five!"

*   *   *

Little Roberta's alibi for missing school for a week was not convincing, but at least it was original. She explained to her teacher, "I had intentional flu."

*   *   *

"What do you like best in kindergarten?"

"Hot Scotch."

"Me slept with daddy last night," said the small child to the kindergarten teacher.

"*I* slept with daddy last night," the teacher corrected.

"Well, then," said the child, "it must have been after me went to sleep."

*　　*　　*

SCHOOL DAZE

Brendan was a slow student, so the teacher decided to use the psychology of personal competitiveness to get him to improve. "You must study harder," she said. "How would you like to stay back in this class and have little Joan go ahead of you?"

"Oh," replied Brendan, "I guess there'll be other Joans."

* * *

"And why, Raymond, do you think your daddy is kind to animals?"

"Well he told us, teacher, that he'd like to kill the man who scratches horses."

Teacher: Keith, why are you late?
Keith: Sorry, teacher. It was late when I started from home.
Teacher: Then why didn't you start early?
Keith: But teacher—by that time it was too late to start early!

* * *

"Now, Henry," said the teacher, "if the phone were to ring in the middle of the night at your home what might it mean?"

"The bill is paid."

* * *

The child was explaining why he preferred to sit in the rear seat of the last row in the classroom. "Sitting there I get last chance at a question. By then it's almost impossible to guess wrong."

* * *

Scott, age eight, was being taught the proper way to ask a girl for a dance by Miss Benson in a dance instruction class.

A half-hour later, Scott asked the teacher, "Now, how do I get rid of her?"

Two first-graders were standing outside a school one morning. "Do you think," asked one, "that thermonuclear projectiles will pierce the sound barrier?"

"No," said the second. "Once a force enters the substratosphere . . ."

Then the bell rang. "There goes the bell," said the first. "Now we gotta go in and string beads."

*　　*　　*

Teacher: Davie, this homework looks like your father's handwriting!

Davie: Sure, I used his fountain pen!

*　　*　　*

On the first day of school, Mr. Ferris warned his pupils about the dangers of riding their bicycles along the highway. "You must be very careful of traffic," he said. "When I was your age, I had a brand-new bike. A car barely touched it, but I was injured so badly that I never rode again."

There was a hushed silence—then a hand went up. "Please, sir," one of the pupils asked politely, "what did you do with the bike?"

Teacher: Giles, how much is three times three?

Giles: Nine?

Teacher: That's pretty good.

Giles: Pretty good? Say, it's perfect!

* * *

Student Adam Perlmutter, whose father Sam is the well-known Los Angeles attorney, tells about the truant officer who spotted the schoolboy coming out of the picture show.

"Have you missed school lately?" he asked politely.

"Not a bit," said the boy.

* * *

The teacher was questioning Donnie. "If a number of cattle is called a herd, and a number of sheep a flock, what would a number of camels be called?"

"A carton," he replied.

* * *

Teacher: What, in your opinion, is the height of stupidity?

Kid: How tall are you?

Teacher: At your age I could name all the Presidents—and in the proper order.

Wesley: Yes, but then there were only three or four of them.

* * *

The tough kid was getting an eye examination in school. "Read what you see on that chart," said the teacher.

"Okay," he said. "I read it."

"Read it aloud."

"Whatsa matter?" he asked. "Can't you read?"

* * *

During a grammar lesson one day, Miss Dressel wrote on the blackboard, "I didn't have no fun at the seashore."

Then she turned to the class and said to one of the pupils, "Roy, how should I correct this?"

"Get a boyfriend," he answered.

The children brought Christmas gifts to Miss Brown. She decided to try and guess what they were.

Martin's father had a liquor store. She noticed the package was leaking and tasted it. "Did you bring me some scotch?"

"No, teacher!" said Martin.

Leon's dad had a florist shop. She said to him, "Did you bring me flowers?"

"Yes, teacher!" answered Leon.

She then went back to the leaking package and tasted it again. "Martin, did you bring me rum?"

"No, teacher!"

Donald's father had a candy store. She asked him, "Have you brought me some candy?"

"Yes, teacher!" replied Donald.

She then went back to the package and tasted the leak again. "Martin, did you bring me some gin?"

"No, teacher," said the child. "I brought you a puppy!"

Teacher: Now, Brian, if I lay two eggs here and three over there, how many will there be all together?

Brian: Personally, I don't think you could do it.

* * *

A seven-year-old told his teacher, "I don't want to scare you, but my daddy says that if I don't get better grades, somebody's going to get spanked!"

* * *

"What are you doing home?"

"I put a stick of dynamite under the teacher's desk."

"You march right back to school and apologize!"

"What school?"

* * *

Teacher: What is wind?
Mona: Air in a hurry!

Little Lester came to school one day just bubbling over with his new information. "I'm going to have a baby brother," he told his teacher.

"How do you know it's going to be a brother?" she asked.

"Well, do you remember last time my mother was sick, and I got a little baby sister?"

"Yes."

"Well, his time my daddy is sick."

*   *   *

Teacher: Name five things that contain milk.

Phillip: Butter, cheese, ice cream . . . and . . . two cows.

*   *   *

Miss Collins had been reading to her class about the rhinoceros family. "Now name some things," she said, "that are very dangerous to get near to, and that have horns."

"Automobiles," answered Arthur.

Jimmy Zezas, Wyoming's youngest cowpoke, gets belly laughs with this lollapalooza:

One rainy day the kindergarten teacher spent over half an hour pulling galoshes onto wet little feet, getting the children ready to go home. When she came to Barry, it took several minutes to maneuver him into his galoshes. Finally they were on.

"Thank you," said Barry. "You know, these galoshes aren't mine."

The poor teacher moaned, sat Barry down again and pulled and pulled until his galoshes came off again. "Now then," she asked, "to whom do these galoshes belong?"

"My brother," explained Barry. "But my mother makes me wear them anyhow."

Reggie came home from school and said to his mother, "Our teacher is really dumb. For four days she has asked us how much two and two is. We told her it was four. But she still doesn't know it; this morning she asked again!"

*   *   *

Marvin raised his hand for permission to go out, but Miss Grant said, "As soon as we finish this lesson, Marvin."

A minute later Richie, seated right in back of Marvin, raised his hand.

"I suppose you want permission to leave the room, too," said the teacher.

"No, I don't," replied Richie, "I just want to second the motion for Marvin."

*   *   *

Marcia was very downcast at school when she was told the date was March first. "I've just learned how to spell February," she explained, "and now it's gone."

Little Al: I don't like what you said and I'll give you five minutes to take it back.

Big Milton: Yeah, and what if I don't take it back in five minutes?

Little Al: Well, then I'll give you longer.

* * *

The class was having a lesson in geography and the teacher asked, "Gregory, where's the largest corn grown?"

"On Pop's little toe!"

* * *

The father asked his son, "Have you been a good boy at school today?"

"I sure was," the boy replied. "You can't get into much trouble when you're standing in the corner all day."

* * *

Big Brother: Well, Rex, how do you like school?

Rex: Closed!

Marc went to a school picnic and had a terrible time. He was stung by a bee; he fell into a creek; a little girl pulled his hair; he got badly sunburned.

He arrived home, limping and with torn and muddy clothes. "Well, son," greeted his mother, "what kind of time did you have at the picnic?"

"Mom," he replied, "I'm so glad I'm back, I'm glad I went."

*　　*　　*

SCHOOL

A place where children go to catch cold from other children so they can stay home.

*　　*　　*

"Now, class, are there any questions?"

"Yes, where do those words go when you rub them off the blackboard?"

*　　*　　*

"In what battle did General Wolfe cry, 'I die happy!'?"

"In his last battle."

Teacher: (answering the phone): You say Gary Gage has a bad cold and can't come to school? Who is this speaking?

Voice: This is my father.

* * *

A girl in the third grade was having trouble doing her arithmetic without counting on her fingers, so her mother tried to teach her to do sums in her head.

"Close your eyes and imagine you see a blackboard," the mother told her. "Do you see it?"

"Yes," said the girl.

"Now write your problem on it. Do you have it written down?"

"Not yet," the girl said, "I can't find the chalk!"

* * *

The teacher asked her pupils, "Cleanliness is next to—what?"

"Impossible!" answered little Arnold.

Carl was assigned to write a composition entitled, "Where I Came From." When he returned home from school, he entered the kitchen where his mother was preparing dinner.

"Where did I come from, mama?" he asked.

"The stork brought you."

"And where did daddy come from?"

"The stork brought him, too."

"And what about grandpa?"

"Why, the stork brought him too, darling."

Carl very carefully made notes on what mama had told him, and the next day he handed in the following composition:

"According to my calculations, there hasn't been a natural birth in my family for the past three generations."

The teacher asked Jules, "Was George Washington a soldier or a sailor?"

"A soldier," said the boy.

"How do you know?"

"I've seen a picture of him crossing the Delaware River, and no sailor would stand up in a boat like that!"

*　　*　　*

The grammar school class was studying the alphabet.

"What comes after T?" the teacher asked.

A little girl quickly answered, "V."

*　　*　　*

All the pupils in a third-grade classroom were asked to draw pictures of what they wanted to be when they grew up. One boy drew himself as a pilot. Another drew himself at the wheel of a fire engine. But little Agnes turned in a blank piece of paper.

When the teacher asked why, Agnes explained, "I want to be married—but I don't know how to draw it."

Teacher: I hope I didn't see you looking at someone else's paper, Billy.

Billy: I hope so, too, teacher.

* * *

Five-year-old Gerald rushed home from kindergarten and begged his mother to buy him a pair of six-shooters.

"What for?" asked his mother. "Surely you don't need those guns for school?"

"I sure do," said Gerald. "Teacher said that tomorrow she's going to teach us how to draw."

* * *

STORKS AND SIBLINGS

A seven-year-old from a large family was told by the nurse that the stork had left him another baby sister. "Would you like to see her?" asked the nurse.

"I've seen lots of babies, so I don't care," said the boy. "But if it's okay, I'd sure like to see the stork!"

* * *

Five-year-old Chris came home from a birthday party. "I'm never going to believe another word you say," he told his mother. "I was the only kid at the party who didn't know that babies are brought by the stork!"

Isabelle sat in her doctor's waiting room, alongside of a mother and her child of five. The child sat very quietly while Isabelle and the mother exchanged pleasantries. Isabelle was impressed by the child's good behavior.

"I wish," she said, "I had a little boy like you."

"Well," said the child, "why don't you get pregnant?"

* * *

"Mama," asked Egbert as he watched the circus parade, "where do elephants come from? And don't give me that stork routine again!"

* * *

"I sure want a brother or a sister," said a little girl to her uncle, "because I'm all alone."

"Have you asked your folks for one?" he inquired.

"Yes, I did. Mommy said 'Yes' and daddy said 'Yes' too."

"Well, then I'll just bet you have a new baby at your house one of these days."

"Maybe," she sighed. "But I guess God can say 'No.'"

One day five-year-old Elliot got to wondering why his aunt, who'd been married for a couple of years, didn't have any children. He asked her and she said, "I've been looking for a baby in the cabbage patch, but I haven't found one yet."

"Well," said Elliot, "if that's how you go about it, no wonder you haven't had any luck."

* * *

A four-year-old girl asked her five-year-old brother, "Where do babies come from?"

"Babies," he said, "come from heaven, of course."

"If babies come from heaven," she asked, "why did Mommy have to go to the hospital?"

There was a long pause then the boy said, "To get their skins put on."

* * *

One boy told his friends exactly how God creates people: "He draws us first, then cuts us out."

* * *

"If my mom wasn't looking," said a little lad, "I'd sell my brother!"

A boy cornered his reluctant dad one day and asked, "Dad, where did I come from?"

The father told all, while the boy squirmed and fidgeted. When it was over, the father said, "Tell me, son, what made you ask where you came from?"

"Well, the new kid across the street says he comes from Ohio—and I wanted to know where I came from."

* * *

"Why can't we have a baby?" Bert asked his mother.

"They cost too much," she said.

"How much do they cost?"

"About three hundred dollars."

"But," said the boy, "that's not much, considering how long they last!"

* * *

"Do you help your mother with your brand-new brother?"

"I sure do," replied four-year-old Maurice.

"How?"

"I put on the powder."

"What's the most important thing to remember about that?"

"Get it on the right end."

41

A little boy answered the phone. "Hello?"

"Hello. Is your mother there?"

"No, she isn't home."

"How about your father?"

"Not home either."

"Who is home?"

"My sister."

"Will you call your sister?"

"Okay." ... [delay] ... "I'm sorry, but you can't talk to her."

"Why not?"

"I can't get her out of the crib."

*   *   *

A mother had just brought her newborn triplets home from the hospital.

Her older boy, a five-year-old, took his first look at the new babies and said, "We'd better start calling folks. They're going to be a lot harder to get rid of than kittens."

*   *   *

Four-year-old Russ watched as his mother put a fresh diaper on his baby brother. When she neglected to dust the infant with talcum powder, the boy shouted, "Hold it, mom! You forgot to salt him!"

"How many children in your family?" asked the nursery school teacher of a four-year-old.

"There are seven of us."

"That must cost a lot of money."

"Oh, no. We don't buy babies, we raise 'em."

*　*　*

Mimi Brenner, the bubbling Brooklyn homemaker, tells about the four-year-old boy who brought a puppy to visit his grandmother. She was busy fixing dinner and paid no attention to the pup.

After a while the boy, his eyes filling with tears, asked her, "Aren't you even going to speak to your grand-dog?"

*　*　*

Father had just informed Junior that there would soon be a playmate for him in the house. Junior did not quite comprehend. That's when his mother stepped in.

"Which would you prefer, darling?" asked his mom, "a baby sister or brother?"

"If you think you could handle it, ma, I'd much rather have a pony."

Harker asked his nine-year-old nephew if his two-year-old brother had started to talk yet.

"Why should he talk?" the kid asked. "He gets everything he wants by hollering."

*   *   *

Alison Spritzler, whose father Ramon is a top Los Angeles internist, broke up dad's friends with this bauble:

Five-year-old Rick had a terrible habit of sucking his thumb; a habit his mother had been trying desperately to break.

"One of these days," she told him, "if you keep on sucking your thumb, you're going to blow up and burst!"

A few days later, his mother's bridge club came over. One of the women was very much in the family way. Rick wandered into the room, and pointed at the pregnant woman. "Say," he shouted, "I know what you've been doing!"

*   *   *

FOUR-LEGGED AND FLYING
FURRY FRIENDS

A young city dog met an older acquaintance at a friendly fire hydrant. "What's your name?" asked the acquaintance.

"I'm not quite sure," admitted the city dog, "but I think it's Down Boy."

*　　*　　*

Did you hear about the dog who went to the flea circus and stole the whole show?

A well-meaning lady held a cookie above a dog and commanded, "Speak! Speak!"

"Why," said the dog modestly, "I hardly know what to say!"

* * *

Two flies met in a grocery store.

"Well, hello, Mrs. Buzz," said one. "I haven't seen you in ages. How's everything with you?"

"Not so good," replied her friend. "Junior's been so cranky, I've had to walk the ceiling with him every night this week."

* * *

Marilyn Mitchell, the merry Tarzana homemaker, suggested this bit of mad monkeyshines:

It was getting cold and all the other pigeons had flown south, but Baby Pigeon could not seem to fly. One day Mama Pigeon said, "If you don't learn to fly today, I'll have to tie a rope around your neck and tow you along."

At that, Baby Pigeon cried, "But mommy, I don't want to be pigeon-towed."

* * *

Do you know why a humming bird hums? Because he doesn't know the words.

A baby caterpillar was watching a moth in flight directly above him.

"By heaven," he vowed. "They'll never get me up in one of those contraptions."

*   *   *

KANGAROO

A great big mouse with a pocket in its stomach

*   *   *

"I certainly hope it doesn't rain today," one lady kangaroo remarked to another. "I just hate it when the children have to play inside."

*   *   *

A shark appeared at a convention of deep-sea denizens with two very small fish swimming directly beneath him. The whale in charge of the convention became curious.

"Look," he said, "I understand the function of one of those little fish you have with you. He's the pilot fish. But what's the other one?"

"Oh," replied the shark, "he's the co-pilot."

Los Angeles laughter lover Samantha Mills likes this little lampoon:

Mama and Papa Turtle were talking about their kids catching cold because their necks stuck out of their shells.

"Stop worrying," advised Papa. "We'll buy them one of those people-necked sweaters."

* * *

Two turtles decided to stop in for a soda. After they entered the drugstore, it began to rain. The big turtle said to the little turtle, "Go home and get the umbrella."

"I will," agreed the little turtle, "if you promise not to drink my soda."

Two years later the big turtle thought, "I guess he is never coming back. I may as well drink his soda."

As he reached for the other glass, a voice from outside the door called, "If you touch that soda, I won't go home and get the umbrella."

* * *

Said the twin calf to the mother cow,
"Shoot the udder to me, mudder,
"Shoot the udder udder to me brudder,
"What's the matter, mudder, don't you
    know one udder from the udder?"

Did you hear about the farmer who crossed a cow with an octopus and got a do-it-yourself dairy?

* * *

FARM PHILOSOPHY

Never milk a cow during a thunderstorm. She may be struck by lightning—and you'll be left holding the bag.

* * *

There once was a man who loved the bees
He always was their friend,
He liked to sit upon their hives
But they stung him in the end.

* * *

There were two young sheep grazing in a meadow. "Baa-aa-aaa," said the first sheep.

"Moooooo," said the second sheep.

"What do you mean, 'Moooooo'?" asked the first.

"I'm studying a foreign language," explained the second.

* * *

Did you hear about the two corpuscles who loved in vein?

Three camels were walking through the desert. After six days of unbearable heat, one camel turned to the others and said, "The heck with my reputation—I'm thirsty!"

* * *

There were three ostriches. Two of them heard a strange noise and quickly buried their heads in the sand.

The third ostrich looked around and said, "Where is everybody?"

* * *

Know how porcupines make love?
V-e-r-y c-a-r-e-f-u-l-l-y.

* * *

"Ask me if I'm a rabbit."
"Are you a rabbit?"
"Yes. Now ask me if I'm an antelope."
"Are you an antelope?"
"No, stupid. I already told you I was a rabbit!"

* * *

The birds and the bees must have it tuff
When their babies start asking stuff.

Mother Lion: What are you doing?
Baby Lion: I'm chasing a hunter around a tree.
Mother Lion: How many times have I told you not play with your food?

*   *   *

If an elephant didn't have a trunk, how would he smell?

Trunk or no trunk, he'd still smell terrible.

*   *   *

How do you make an elephant float?

Two scoops of ice cream, soda, and some elephant.

*   *   *

What can you tell about three elephants walking down the street wearing pink sweatshirts?

They're all on the same team.

*   *   *

What's red and white on the outside and gray and white on the inside?

Campbell's Cream of Elephant Soup.

Mort Fleischmann, RCA's popular West Coast exec in charge of news and information, gets guffaws from nieces and nephews with this golden gag:

Leonard the lion was stalking through the jungle looking for trouble. He grabbed a passing giraffe and asked, "Who is the king of the jungle?"

"You are, O Mighty Lion," answered the giraffe.

Leonard then grabbed a tiger and asked, "Who is king of the jungle?"

"You are, O Mighty Lion," replied the tiger.

Next Leonard met an elephant and asked, "Who is the king of the jungle?"

The elephant grabbed him with his trunk, whirled him around, and threw him against a tree, leaving the lion in a crumpled heap on the ground.

Leonard struggled to his feet. "Hey," he said, "just because you don't know the answer is no reason for getting so rough!"

Why do elephants have squinting eyes?
From reading the small print on peanut packages.

*   *   *

Why do elephants have white tusks?
They use Crest.

*   *   *

Why did the eleph marry the ant?
He wanted to have Eleph-ants.

*   *   *

Why did the elephant and the donkey fight?
It was an election year!

*   *   *

Why do elephants' tusks stick way out?
Because their parents won't allow them to get braces.

*   *   *

What's the difference between an elephant and a flea?
An elephant can have fleas but a flea can't have elephants.

Once upon a time there were three bears,
Papa Bear, Mama Bear, and Baby Bear.

Papa Bear   (early one morning) : Some-
                 one's been eating my por-
                 ridge.

Baby Bear: Someone's been eating my
                 porridge, too.

Mama Bear: Gripe! Gripe! Gripe! I
                 haven't even put it on the
                 table yet.

*   *   *

A woman in a theater couldn't see the
movie because of the huge man sitting
ahead of her in a bearskin coat. She tried
peering around the giant. To her surprise,
she discovered that it was a huge bear.
She leaned over and tapped the man sitting
next to the bear.

"Do you know there's a bear sitting next
to you?" she asked.

"Yes," replied the man. "He's with me."

The puzzled woman thought for a mo-
ment, then nudged the man again. "Is he
enjoying the movie?"

"I don't know," said the man, "but he
loved the book."

*   *   *

ALL GOD'S CHILLUN

Natalie, frightened by an electrical storm, tried to sit still while her parents reassured her. Suddenly there was an extra-loud thunderclap.

The girl walked to the screen door and shouted, "That's enough, God . . . cut it out!"

*　　*　　*

A pastor, welcoming a new family into the area, patted three-year-old Denise on the head and said, "God bless you."

"Why did he say that?" said the girl to her mother. "I didn't sneeze."

After five-year-old Matt gave a loud whistle in the middle of the minister's sermon, his grandmother launched into a scolding.

"Why on earth would you do such a thing?" she demanded.

"I've been praying for a long time that God would teach me to whistle," he explained, "and this morning He did."

* * *

A family visited the West Coast and went out to the beach on a foggy day to see the Pacific.

They arrived at low tide and the fog was so murky that the water was hidden from view.

"Don't worry," said their son, "we'll see the ocean as soon as God fills it up."

* * *

Alonzo devoted an entire rainy indoors afternoon to a drawing he was doing with varicolored crayons. His mother finally looked over his shoulder and asked, "Who's that you're drawing, son?"

"God," answered the boy.

"Don't be silly," said his mother. "Nobody knows what God looks like."

"Well," said the youngster, "they will when I'm finished."

Five-year-old Doug kept staring across the aisle one morning in church at a handsome young man with a flowing beard.

Finally, he told his grandmother, "I want to go over and sit with Jesus."

* * *

A boy who'd been spanked by his father for making too much noise climbed into his mother's lap and said, "Mama, I wish you had married Jesus. He loves little children!"

* * *

Told that the Savior lives inside us, Robin refused a drink of water after class, explaining, "I don't wanna drown Jesus."

* * *

Four-year-old Dick figured out how to take a family dispute to a higher court. He wanted to go barefoot on the first warm day in spring, but his parents wouldn't let him.

At breakfast the next morning, he said, "I can go barefoot today. I asked Jesus about it last night and He said, 'Yes, Dick, you can go barefoot. It's all right.' And, you know, Jesus always knows what's best."

Marci assured her mother that she'd said her prayers the night before, but added, "They were different, 'cause when I got on my knees I began thinking that God hears the same old stuff every night— so I told Him the story of The Three Bears instead!"

* * *

Little Paula prayed for a thousand new dolls for her birthday. When she didn't get them, her dad said, "I guess God didn't answer your prayers."

"Oh, yes, he did," answered the girl. "He said, 'No.' "

* * *

"Don't forget to include grandma in your prayers," the mother said to her daughter. "Ask God to bless her and let her live to be very, very old."

"Oh, she's old enough," the girl said. "I'd rather ask God to make her younger."

* * *

A two-and-a-half-year-old who hadn't said her prayers for several days finally announced, "I want to say my prayers tonight. Won't God be surprised?"

"... and God bless Mommy and Daddy but
don't send them any more children—
they don't know how to handle
what they've already got."

A sleepy little girl barely stayed awake long enough to hear her big sister's goodnight to God. Then, nodding and yawning, she whispered, "Dear God, my prayer is the same as hers. Amen."

* * *

Three-year-old Laurie was delighted with the reception she got at church. She told her mother, "They sang a whole song just for me . . . 'Laurie, Laurie, Hallelujah.'"

* * *

Charlie came skipping into the house with a big lollipop in his hands. "Where did you get it?" his mother asked.

"I bought it with the nickel you gave me."

"The nickel I gave you was for Sunday school."

"I know, mom," said the boy, "but the minister met me at the door and got me in free."

* * *

A girl asked why it was that Jesus wore long hair. Before the teacher could think of an answer, another little girl said, "Only His hairdresser knows."

Janet returned from her first Catholic service and told her mother, "It was so hot in that church today that the priest had to walk down the aisle and sprinkle us all with water."

*   *   *

That day, Mrs. Kendrick was distraught with her two children. While at the dinner table, she suddenly looked up and sighed, "Oh, Lord, help me with these children."

Immediately, four-year-old Donna bowed her head and was silent. Mrs. Kendrick was delighted, thinking her daughter was asking God for help. But then Donna looked up at her and said, "I just asked Him *not* to help you."

*   *   *

Aunt Dierdre took her nephew to church. As they approached the pew, she whispered to him, "Can you genuflect?"

"No," he said, "but I can somersault."

*   *   *

A four-year-old watched carefully as parishioners dropped their cash in the plate, and then warned his father, "Don't pay for me, dad ... remember, I'm under five."

Bob Padilla, the West Coast's consummate wood craftsman, came up with this comical coup:

Four-year-old Mike was warned by his older sister that he wouldn't be allowed to talk in church.

"They just won't let you say a word," she said.

"Who won't?" asked Michael.

"The hushers," she replied.

* * *

A mother gave her small daughter three dimes to put in the plate as it came by. The child looked at the three coins and asked, "Is this lunch money for Jesus, Mary, and Joseph?"

* * *

Taken to church for the first time, four-year-old Jean was mystified when the entire congregation kneeled. "What are they doing?" she asked her mother.

"S-s-sh," whispered the mother. "They're praying."

"What?" exclaimed Jean. "With their clothes on?"

Three-year-old Victor was intrigued by the Communion rite and watched every move of the priest until he finished by wiping the chalice.

Then the boy turned to his mother and said, "He's doing dishes, mom . . . now can we go home?"

* * *

A boy came home and told his father why his gym teacher insisted he dry and powder his feet after every shower. "It's so we won't get Catholic's foot."

* * *

Dan Cinelli, the dapper New York ex-cabbie, tells about the two sisters, Cora and Diane, who were in a restaurant. Before the meal, little Diane prepared to bless herself. Cora nudged her.

"You don't have to say grace, Diane. We're paying for this."

* * *

"Can you tell me what grace is, son?"

"No, sir."

"Surely you can. Your father says it before each meal."

"Oh, yes. It's 'Go easy on the butter, it costs ninety cents a pound.' "

Tough Kid: Hey, ma, is it true that the Lord gives us our daily bread?

Mother: Certainly.

Kid: And that Santa Claus brings us clothes and toys?

Mother: Yes.

Kid: Does the stork bring babies?

Mother: Of course.

Kid: Then why don't you let me bump off the old man, we don't need him!

*   *   *

MISCHIEF MAKERS

At dinner Mario said to his dad, "My two buddies and I helped a little old lady cross the street."

"That was very nice," said his father. "But why did it take three of you to help her across the street?"

"She didn't want to go!"

*　　*　　*

"You little roughneck!" shouted an irate woman from her backyard, "I'll teach you to throw rocks at my dog!"

"Thanks lady!" said the young boy, "I could use a few lessons!"

67

Tommy:	I always do a good deed every day.
Aunt Jane:	That's fine. What good deed have you done today?
Tommy:	Why, there was only castor oil enough for one of us this morning, so I let my little brother have it.

*   *   *

Jackie Lewerke, the Los Angeles dinner party hostess extraordinaire, loves this laughable lump of lunacy:

Nine-year-old Nancy stood by the gate in front of her house looking into the street. In a while, a well-dressed man came by.

"Hey, mister," she said, "mind opening the gate for me?"

"Sure!" he said and pushed the gate open. "Tell me, why couldn't you do it yourself?" he asked.

"Wet paint," said the girl.

*   *   *

Newsboy:	Extra! Extra! Read all about it—two men swindled.
Man:	Give me a paper, boy. Say, there isn't anything about two men being swindled.
Newsboy:	Extra! Extra! Three men swindled.

An alarmed motorist stopped hurriedly when he saw a young fellow standing beside a small overturned sports car.

"Anybody hurt in the accident?" he asked.

"There was no accident," replied the youth calmly. "I'm changing a tire."

* * *

"I'm really not wealthy, and I don't have a yacht and a convertible like Walter Warren," apologized the young man. "But, baby, I love you."

"And I love you, too," replied the girl. "But tell me more about Walter."

* * *

Amanda wanted to marry Timmy, but her mother absolutely refused to allow the match.

"Sorry, Timmy," said the girl, "but my mother thinks you're too feminine!"

"That's all right," said Timmy, "compared to her, I probably am!"

TOPSY-TURVY TEENS

Boy   (with one hand cupped over the other): If you can guess what I have in my hand, I'll take you out tonight.

Girl: An elephant!

Boy: Nope! But that's close enough. I'll pick you up at 7:30.

*   *   *

TEENAGERS

People who think curbing their emotions means parking by the roadside.

77

Three young kids were reading magazines while waiting in the pediatrician's office. When the doctor called the first boy in for his examination, he noticed he was reading *Popular Science* and asked, "What do you want to be when you grow up? A scientist?"

"I want to be an astronaut," replied the boy.

When it was the second boy's turn, the doctor noticed he was reading *Field and Stream* and said, "You probably are going to be a fisherman when you grow up— right?"

"I wanna be a fishing-boat captain," said the second boy.

When it was the third boy's turn the pediatrician noticed he was looking at a *Playboy* centerfold. "What are you going to be when you grow up?" asked the M.D.

"I don't know," said the boy, "but I can't wait to get started."

*   *   *

Mrs. Crawford offered to care for Kathleen, the eight-year-old daughter of her next-door neighbor. She arrived in time to prepare breakfast, laying a generous helping of bacon and eggs in front of the child.

"Mother always has hot biscuits for breakfast," said Kathleen.

So Mrs. Crawford, anxious to oblige, hurried into the kitchen and quickly prepared a plate of hot biscuits which she laid in front of the girl. "No, thank you," she said.

"But I thought you said your mother always has hot biscuits for breakfast?" asked the surprised woman.

"She does," said the eight-year-old. "But I don't eat them."

* * *

The revenue man stopped the little hillbilly boy.

"Son," he said, "I'll give you a dollar if you take me to see your father's still."

"I'll take you," agreed the little boy. "But you'll have to give me the dollar first."

"No," insisted the revenuer. "When I get back I'll give it to you."

"Look, mister," said the kid. "If I take you to my old man's still, you ain't comin' back."

69

Harry went to see his girlfriend Rita after a long absence.

As luck would have it, her little brother Emil was seated in front of the television set watching his favorite western. Annoyed by the little brat's presence, Harry decided to use some child psychology on him.

"Emil," he suggested, "look outside the window and for every man you see wearing a red hat, I'll give you fifty cents."

"Sounds great," said Emil. Then he ran upstairs to look out the window.

Ten minutes later, while Harry and Rita were getting reacquainted, Emil suddenly rushed into the room.

"Didn't I tell you to watch for men with red hats?" shouted Harry.

"But I did," explained the boy, "and while you were talking to my sister, a Shriners' parade passed by. At fifty cents a head, you owe me twelve hundred dollars!"

Young Greg greeted his sister's boyfriend enthusiastically. "That harmonica you gave me for my birthday is absolutely the best present I've ever had."

"I'm glad you like it."

"Yes, mother gives me a quarter a week not to play it."

*   *   *

Salesman: Sonny, is your mother at home?

Sammy: Yes, sir.

Salesman: (after knocking for some time and getting no answer): I thought you said she was at home?

Sammy: Yes, sir, but I don't live here.

*   *   *

Note found in a Wisconsin household, penciled by a nine year-old girl after an argument:

"Goodbye family. You all hate me. I love you anyhow. Bless you!

"P. S. In case of fire, I'm in the attic."

Lovable Linda Yates, the Superscope exec, likes this lesson in latent honesty:

Little Kit was taken by his mother to a seance, and on being asked by the medium if there was anyone he would like to speak to, said, "My grandpa."

Shortly afterwards the medium went into a suitable trance and soon a spooky voice came floating through the air: "This is grandpa speaking from heaven—what is it you would like to know, my boy?"

"Hello, grandpa," said Kit. "What are you doing in heaven? You're not even dead yet!"

* * *

A kindly senior citizen was strolling down the street when he noticed a small boy standing on the front steps of a house trying to reach the doorbell.

The boy stood on tiptoe, even jumped up as high as he could, but was unable to reach the bell.

The old man walked up the stairs, rang the bell and said, "Well, little fella, what now?"

"I don't know what you're gonna do," said the boy, "but I'm gonna run!"

Nancy Medwig, the pretty Pittsburgh exec secretary, produced this perfect plum of persiflage:

Robinson rushed off a train and ran up to a little boy standing on the platform.

"We've only got a short stop here," he said. "Here's a dollar. Go in that lunchroom and get me a sandwich, will you? And here's another buck. Get a sandwich for yourself, too."

The boy was gone so long Robinson began to get nervous. Just as the conductor hollered, "All 'board!" the kid dashed out of the lunchroom and ran over to the man.

"Here's your dollar," he said, swallowing a mouthful. "They only had one sandwich."

Short-haired girl to long-haired lad: "Of course daddy doesn't mind our being alone together every night. He thinks you're a girl!"

*　*　*

Steve, who fancied himself a lover, tinkered with his car a little before he took Teresa, the town beauty, out for a ride. And when the two reached the crest of a local hill, in full view of the shining, romantic moon, the car's engine started to knock.

"I wonder," said Steve, "what that knock could be."

"I'll tell you one thing," said Teresa. "It's not opportunity."

*　*　*

Micky: I'm through with that girl.
Nicky: Oh, why?
Micky: She asked me if I could dance.
Nicky: Well, what's wrong with that?
Micky: I was dancing with her when she asked.

When fourteen-year-old Marsha returned home from a party, her mother asked her how she'd enjoyed it.

"It was all right," she said, "except a couple of boys got into a fight over dancing with me."

"Really!" replied the mother, pleased at her daughter's apparent popularity. "What happened?"

"Well, the fight started when one of them punched the other in the side with his elbow and said, 'You dance with her,' and then the other one punched him back and said, 'No! You dance with her.'"

I want a girl just like the girl
that turned down dear old dad

*   *   *

He held her close as the music drifted into a waltz. They didn't speak until the lovely strains ended. Then she gazed up and whispered, "This dance really makes me long for another."

"Yeah," he replied, "me too. But she couldn't come."

*   *   *

Joe: What's so unusual about your girl-friend?
Moe: She chews on her nails.
Joe: Lots of girls chew on their nails.
Moe: Toenails?

*   *   *

When a boy breaks a date, he usually has to.

When a girl breaks a date, she usually has two.

Randy Marks, the University of Hartford glamour queen, came up with this comical cackler:

A New England youth went to see his girlfriend one night. They sat in the parlor, with the firelight flickering romantically over the girl's lovely face. Finally the guy got up enough courage to ask, "Prudence, will you marry me?"

"Yes, Eddie."

About an hour passed by in complete silence. Then Prudence asked, "Eddie, why don't you say something?"

The New England youth looked at her mournfully. "Well," he said, "I think I've talked too much already."

* * *

DANCING DIALOGUE

Boy: What would I have to give you for one little kiss?

Girl: Chloroform!

* * *

One teenage girl told another, "I developed an entirely new personality yesterday, but my father made me wash it off."

TEENAGE

*The time between pigtails and
cocktails*

* * *

"If I refuse to marry you," asked the sweet young thing, "will you really commit suicide?"

"That's what I usually do in these cases."

* * *

Boy: Will you marry me?
Girl: No, but I'll always admire your good taste.

* * *

Paul had just proposed marriage to his lady love and she had turned him down. "If you don't marry me immediately," he threatened, "I'll go to the lake, cut a hole in the ice, dive in and drown myself."

"Why this is April. The ice won't cover the lake for eight months!"

"Okay, then I'll wait."

"What would you say if I asked you to marry me?"

"Nothing. I can't talk and laugh at the same time."

* * *

Eskimo Boy: What would you say if I told you I had come through a hundred miles of ice and snow just to tell you I love you?

Eskimo Girl: I'd say that was a lot of mush.

* * *

"Pop, I've raised that two dollars I've needed for so long."

"Good work, son. A boy worth his salt should try as early as possible to make himself independent of his father and stand on his own feet. How did you do it?"

"Borrowed it from Mom."

TEENAGE

*The time when a girl makes up her
face more easily than her mind*

* * *

After a blind date a fellow mentioned to
his friend, "When I got home last night,
I felt a lump in my throat."

"You really like her, huh?"

"No, she's a karate expert."

* * *

The girl was complaining to her mother,
"I had to change my seat five times at the
movies."

"Some man annoy you?"

"Yes," said the girl. "Finally!"

* * *

Pru: He puts on too many airs to suit me.
Sue: I couldn't get him to date me, either.

Boy: Ah, look at the cow and the calf rubbing noses in the pasture. That sight makes me want to do the same.

Girl: Well, go ahead . . . it's your cow.

* * *

"I'm sorry," said the bored young lady when the drip asked her for another date. "I can't see you Sunday, I'm expecting a headache."

* * *

"You can never tell about men," the sophisticated miss advised her younger sister. "Either they're so slow you want to scream, or so fast you have to."

* * *

It's usually a girl's geography that determines her history.

* * *

SENIOR SONG

She's only a rag, a bone and a hank of hair, but every guy she meets wants to become a junk dealer.

"When I went out with Fred, I had to slap his face five times."

"Was he that fresh?"

"No! I thought he was dead!"

* * *

Tad: Your sister is spoiled, isn't she?

Brad: No, that's the perfume she uses.

* * *

Mother: How could you be so rude to tell your sister she's stupid. Tell her you're sorry.

Boy: Sis, I'm sorry you're stupid.

* * *

"Well, and how are you getting on with your courtship of the banker's daughter?"

"Not so bad. I'm getting some encouragement now."

"Really, is she beginning to loosen up or something?"

"Not exactly, but last night she told me she had said 'No' for the last time."

* * *

He: How about a kiss?

She: Sorry, but I have scruples.

He: That's all right. I've been vaccinated.

88

Floyd: You know, sweetheart, since I met you I can't eat . . . I can't sleep . . . I can't drink . . .

Sandra: Why not?

Floyd: I'm broke!

*   *   *

TEENAGERS

People who regard home as a drive-in where Pop pays for the hamburger

*   *   *

"Without you, everything is dark and dreary . . . the clouds gather and the wind beats the rain . . . then comes the warm sun . . . you are like a rainbow."

"Is this a proposal or a weather report?"

*   *   *

Girl (on doorstep at end of date) : Since we've been going Dutch all evening, you kiss yourself and I'll kiss myself.

*   *   *

My sister always has her own way. She writes her diary a week ahead of time.

Karyl Wildman, the University of Miami beauty, provided this blithe bon mot:

Elroy was having a hard time trying to decide what to give his new girlfriend for her birthday. He wandered around a large department store, looking at various displays, until he spotted the perfume counter.

"I've got to get my girl a birthday present," he said to the clerk. "Would you suggest perfume?"

"Certainly," smiled the woman. "Every girl likes to get a bottle of nice perfume for a gift."

"What kind should I get her?" asked the youth.

"Well," said the saleswoman, "here's a new perfume called 'Maybe.'"

"I don't want 'Maybe,'" replied Elroy. "I want 'Sure Thing'!"

* * *

Harriet, a high school junior, strolled into English class ten minutes late.

"Where've you been?" asked the teacher.

"The boy who was following me walked very slowly," replied Harriet.

Father: What's wrong, Belinda? Usually you talk on the phone for hours. This time you only talked half an hour. How come?

Belinda: It was a wrong number.

* * *

Blossoming sub-deb to an about-to-be ex-boyfriend: "Let me explain it to you this way, Myron; if our romance was on TV I'd be switching channels."

* * *

BLIND DATE

When a boy or girl generally hits the jerk pot

* * *

The star senior football player made his first visit to the bank. When asked to endorse his check, he wrote, "I heartily endorse this check."

* * *

"How come you go steady with Eloise?"
"She's different from other girls."
"How so?"
"She's the only girl who will go with me."

The girl was anxious, but the boy was nervous.

"What would you do if I kissed you?" he asked.

"I'd call my brother," she said.

"How old is he?"

"Two and a half."

*The time when girls begin to powder
and boys begin to puff*

* * *

Senior Scholar: I beg your pardon, but . . .

Stuck-up Soph: No, you've never met me at a dance or a football game. I don't look like the girl you met in Oshkosh. I'm not going your way, and I wouldn't ride with you on a bet. I didn't ever go to school with you, and I'm not waiting for a bus. I'm on my way to meet my date, who weighs 200 pounds and holds an amateur boxing championship. Now, were you going to say something?

Senior Scholar: Yes, darn it. Your pantyhose are slipping.

* * *

What has 730,697,224 pages
and has sold over 4,000,000 copies?
The 16 funny, inane, ridiculous, irreverent,
wacky, zany, and hilarious joke books by

America's #1 best-selling humorist

Larry Wilde